D0776716

Nowhere Near the Line

Nowhere Near the Line

Pain and Possibility in Teaching and Writing

Elizabeth H. Boquet

Utah State University Press
Logan

Published by Utah State University Press
An imprint of University Press of Colorado
5589 Arapahoe Avenue, Suite 206C
Boulder, Colorado 80303

USU Press Current Arguments in Composition

The University Press of Colorado is a proud member of The Association of American University Presses.

The University Press of Colorado is a cooperative publishing enterprise supported, in part, by Adams State University, Colorado State University, Fort Lewis College, Metropolitan State University of Denver, Regis University, University of Colorado, University of Northern Colorado, Utah State University, and Western State Colorado University.

ISBN 978-160732-575-8 (pbk.: alk. paper)
ISBN 978-160732-576-5 (e-book)
DOI: 10.7330/9781607325765

Library of Congress Cataloging-in-Publication Data

Names: Boquet, Elizabeth, 1966– author.
Title: Nowhere near the line : pain and possibility in teaching and writing / Elizabeth H. Boquet.
Description: Logan : Utah State University Press, [2016] | Includes bibliographical references.
Identifiers: LCCN 2016026716| ISBN 9781607325758 (pbk.) | ISBN 9781607325765 (ebook)
Subjects: LCSH: Boquet, Elizabeth, 1966– | Fairfield University—Faculty—Biography. | English teachers—Connecticut—Biography. | College teachers—Connecticut—Biography. | Firearms—Social aspects—United States. | English language—Rhetoric—Study and teaching.
Classification: LCC PR55.B68 A3 2016 | DDC 378.1/2092 [B] —dc23
LC record available at https://lccn.loc.gov/2016026716

for Dan

Contents

Don't be afraid to jump ahead . . . Make the subject of the next sentence different from the subject of the sentence you just put down. Depend on rhythm, tonality, and the music of language to hold things together. It is impossible to write meaningless sequences. In a sense the next thing always belongs. In the world of imagination, all things belong.

—Richard Hugo

PAIN

I quit kindergarten. Not on day one, when Mrs. Navarre gave me my first-ever spanking, because she found me playing in the third-grade yard. With my cousins, the people I played with every day at home. Not on day two, when I had to make do with the fat, clumsy, safety scissors that refused to cooperate with my preferred left hand. But by day three, when I woke up from nap time to find that my seatmate had hacked off one of my perfectly-plaited braids while I slept . . . well, I was done.

With my braid in my left hand and Mrs. Navarre's hand in my right, I marched down to the principal's office that afternoon for the first time, but not the last, and was sent home for the first time, but not the last. It was up to my parents to figure out how to get me back to school, which they did the next day, and how to keep me there, which they did, though it was never a smooth path, even when it appeared relatively straightforward.

On back-to-school day this year, I called my brother to wish him a happy first day. He too is a professor. He has even worse educational tales to tell.

"Can you believe," I asked, "that we have spent our whole lives going back to school, year after year after year?"

"No, I cannot," he said flatly.

"What would you have done," I asked, "if someone had told you, all those years ago, that at fifty-seven you would still be getting up in the morning and going to school?"

He didn't miss a beat. "I would have shot myself," he said.

On the day I began drafting this essay, news alerts were popping up on social media about yet another episode of school violence—this one the <u>mass</u> shooting at Umpqua Community College in Oregon that killed ten people (nine, plus the perpetrator, whom we all should count). Colleagues prefaced their shared Facebook links with "Enough is enough!" and "What can we do?" and "How do we stop this?!"

But it was a remark by Lawrence Schall, President of Oglethorpe University and co-founder of College Presidents for Gun Safety, quoted in an article written by Paul Fain, that stayed with me as I shaped this material into its current form:

> When I was starting College Presidents for Gun Safety, one of the concerns I heard was the idea there were just too many issues on which to articulate an opinion. Where would it stop? Where would we draw the line? In light of this latest tragedy, on a college campus that could have been any of ours, I would say: We are nowhere near the line yet. Let's worry about that one when we get closer. (*Inside Higher Ed*, October 2, 2015)

Here, I walk this line, tracing the overlaps and intersections of my lifelong education around guns and violence, as a student, a teacher, a feminist, a daughter, a wife, a citizen, and across the dislocations and relocations that are part of a life lived in and around school.

The weekend following the Umpqua shooting, with one eye on a storm skirting the East Coast, I stacked and restacked the large plastic bins filled with report cards, yearbooks, and other memorabilia, making sure they were out of our one potential flood zone—a temperamental casement window just to the right of the oil tank. This should have been fast, physical labor but it was instead slow and contemplative, as I couldn't help but paw through the boxes' contents. Every once in a while I came across a note passed in civics class or a high school Playbill signed by a cast and crew. Rarely did I find anything that I wrote for a class or that was in any way part of an academic assignment.

I didn't find, for example, a paper I wrote for my eleventh-grade English class, in which I argued passionately against gun control, one in which I quoted the familiar bumper stickers—"Guns don't kill people. People kill people" and "When guns are outlawed, only outlaws will have guns." My first research paper. It included a real-life interview with, and primary sources provided by, my Great-Uncle Alvin, a former president of the National Rifle Association.

Guns were everywhere as I was growing up—stuck between spare pillows in a bedroom closet; stuffed into a purse; lining the halls of our main family gathering place, Sunnyside, home to my mother's sister, Anse, and her husband, Uncle Bill, an inveterate collector. Uncle Bill had a working Gatlin gun, a shooting range between the house and the cane fields, and a tiny shed where he made his own ammunition. It smelled of unfinished pine and gunpowder and seemed so sensible that my own father bought my brother a reloading machine for Christmas one year and set it up in the attic of our house. Guns were what men bequeathed to each other. I have my grandmother's wedding rings, my brother has my grandfather's rifles. Each bears our family's history.

Other guns circulated like stories, passed from hand to hand, with no proprietary sense, as my husband Dan learned one summer. Cleaning out our garage for bulky trash pick-up day, he found an old revolver tucked in the bottom drawer of a soon-to-be-discarded dresser. We live in Connecticut, home to some of the strictest gun laws in the nation, even before the shootings at Sandy Hook. "Where did this come from?" Dan wanted to know.

As soon as I saw it, I remembered the day I finished packing for the move from south Louisiana to western Pennsylvania, where I was beginning my Ph.D. program. My 1986 Honda

Civic was bursting at the seams, but as I hugged my parents goodbye and folded myself behind the wheel, I made room for one more item, the loaded .32 my dad was handing me, which I slipped just under my seat. No telling how many state lines I crossed with that gun beneath my knees.

I palmed the pistol and told Dan the story. "Is it even registered?" he asked. "Oh, absolutely not," I said. "Absolutely not." A police officer, he took the gun to headquarters the next day and ran it. Not a trace.

The question of the trace animates inquiry for me. I move across landscapes wondering what else happened there, what stories might be told other than the one I am living at that moment, preternaturally conscious of the violence, real and symbolic, that makes any current scene possible. I have a longstanding fascination with the contemporary photographer Sally Mann, whose work "examine[s] the uneasy confluence of past and present, history and memory, life and death" (Hafera 2007, iii). Mann's series *What Remains*, for example, followed from the murder of a fugitive who was tracked onto her family's farm and killed. In this series, she documents the deterioration of her beloved greyhound's corpse, and she travels to a body farm at the University of Tennessee, where researchers study human decomposition. Her landscapes of Civil War battlefields near her Virginia homestead highlight the return to nature of places that were once dramatically populated by bodies in contact and conflict.

On April 25th, 2014, I arrived at Cathedral Academy in the early afternoon, along with nearly a dozen other Fairfield University students and faculty, for the culminating event of our Cathedral Academy/Fairfield University Poetry-in-Schools project, a celebratory reading of poems from the project's chapbook *Ripples on the Water, Poems in My Heart*. Cathedral

Academy is a high-need elementary and middle school in Bridgeport, CT. We had been partnering for over a year on a six-week poetry series that included fourth- through eighth-grade classrooms led in imaginative writing exercises by a team of Fairfield University advanced poetry students and professors, writing center undergraduate and graduate tutors, and first-year writing students. As I entered the multi-purpose room—stage festooned, student artwork strung, kids buzzing—I learned that one of our participating teachers had been called home, to Milford, the town in which I also live.

"Because," her colleague explained to me, "of the lockdown at Jonathan Law High School."

I had heard nothing of a lockdown, even though Dan is a police officer in Milford and Jonathan Law is both in our neighborhood and in his assigned patrol area. I quickly checked my phone. No reassuring text. ("Bomb threat. False alarm," for example, is an all-too-common one.) No missed call or voice-mail. I spotted an empty folding chair on the perimeter of the room and sat to do a quick search of breaking news in Milford. Up popped a grainy photo of a smiling dark-haired young woman trying on a turquoise formal gown. Stabbed in the hall-way, just before the start of classes, the morning of her prom. Additional details as they become available.

POSSIBILITY

The Poetry-in-Schools project is an extension of a Poetry for Peace contest that Fairfield University has sponsored since 2008, through the Writing Center and other partners, as part of the University's Martin Luther King commemoration program-ming. That contest invites students in kindergarten through eighth grade in the Bridgeport and Fairfield school districts to submit poems written in response to the prompt, "What does peace mean to me?" We regularly receive over 1,000 submissions, with entries from nearly every school in both districts. As the event became one of our signature campus–community programs, we wanted to deepen the connections, so my poetry colleague, Carol Ann Davis, and I set out in search of district partners who might be interested in developing a collaborative poetry series.

After five years of successful events, we initiated the Poetry-in-Schools program in the fall of 2012, scanning the Poetry for Peace rosters in search of repeat (and successful) teachers who might be interested in partnering. Unexpectedly, tragically, our first district partnership emerged in the town where Carol Ann's young children were in school, twenty-five miles from Fairfield's campus: Newtown, CT, where on December 12, 2012, twenty children and six adults were shot and killed in Sandy Hook Elementary School.

For six weeks in the spring of 2013, we met on Monday evenings at Hawley School, the *other* elementary school in Newtown, though workshops were open to all third- through sixth-grade students and their parents. Leaping poems, table poems, bubble poems, place poems. As the weeks progressed, poems cross-referenced each other, players appearing as characters in each other's writings; parents, children, and friends composing collaboratively. The title of the resulting collection, *In the Yellowy Green Phase of Spring*, is taken from one of the collaborative "table" poems, a guided writing exercise whose first line begins "From here, I . . ." and whose subsequent lines, all but one, are kept hidden from the other writers as the unfolding lines of poetry are passed from left to right, writer to writer. This title line (like all the lines in the table poems) can't be ascribed to a particular author. It belongs to us all. Here is its poem:

The Great Unknown

From here, I can see the world
We are in the yellowy green phase of spring
Birds fly in the sky a lot during spring
Some people like to write in a journal
I like to write about flying birds
My cat, the fluffiest cat in the world, purred softly on my lap
I saw the flag at the front of the room jerking like a chained bulldog
The umbrella flew open as the wind took it
I wish I could wake up with a few less unknowns

The summer after Newtown—Newtown now not only a place but an event—Carol Ann and I worked with a program for student leaders from Bridgeport high schools. During one workshop, students designed and presented their ideal high school. The first group got up. And then the next. And then the next. Some had maker spaces, community gardens, experiential learning. Others mentioned services and supplies many of us take for granted: technologies, academic support, even more garbage cans so that the schools could be cleaner. And one after the other, they highlighted something no school could do without: Security. Metal detectors. Guards. "More attractive" door locks to replace the chains that wrap around the door handles in some of the main hallways.

When the time came for questions, I asked whether any of them had considered that an ideal high school might be one with no security measures. Students became animated, their responses ranging from incredulous to adamant. Some laughed aloud. Others protested vigorously, emphatically slapping their hands on the desk or their knees. One or two eyed me skeptically, raising an eyebrow at my privilege. A school without security, they seemed certain, would be no place for learning.

The text I received from Dan late in the day on April 25th—
Cathedral Academy Poetry Celebration Day, Jonathan Law High
School Prom Day—was achingly spare. Two words: "Bad day."

The smiling, dark-haired young woman was Maren Sanchez,
the daughter of a friend; Dan was a first responder, accompanying
Maren to the hospital. The ambulance was crowded, and my husband is large, but along he went, squeezing behind the paramed-
ics, scaling the equipment, and finally hanging by a strap from the
ceiling above the gurney as the EMTs worked below, to no avail.

About the young man who killed her: "He was her friend,"
Maren's mother Donna said to me when we spoke. "They've
known each other *for-ev-er*," she said. A point reiterated by a
minister at the memorial service, who said, "Chris and Maren
were friends." And then, "I'm sure she has already forgiven him."
I'm sure she has already forgiven him.

This, in a school with security, an assigned armed police
officer. With routine lockdown drills that presume an AK-47,
hundreds of rounds of ammo, an unauthorized intruder. What
drill is there for two kids who have known each other since the
fourth grade? Through movie nights and skate park parties and
talent shows and beach cookouts? What drill is there for that?

The day Maren was murdered, an email message arrived
in my inbox from Melissa Quan, Fairfield's director of service
learning. She acknowledged this latest episode of school violence and how it had touched me. In the subject line, Melissa
wrote, "Joining you in your mission." In the body of the message, she paraphrased a foundational question from Mary Rose
O'Reilley that I often invoke: "Is it possible to teach English so
that people stop killing each other?"

Melissa's email reflected back to me work that has indeed
become my mission, in many ways without my realizing it, and
has helped me to become more purposeful in both doing and

making visible this work. The power of O'Reilley's question lies in its simplicity, in its directness. The answer must be equally straightforward—for me, for O'Reilley, for my colleagues who partner with me in peaceable work. The answer is yes. It has to be yes. Otherwise, we should all be doing something else.

Our end-of-year writing center staff gathering took place only a few hours after Maren's memorial service. I considered re-scheduling, I considered skipping, I considered attending as though nothing out of the ordinary had happened that day at all. Then, a day or two before the meeting, an opening came in the form of a note from Carol Ann, inviting the writing center staff to do some therapeutic sculpting as part of our semester reflections, using materials from an organization called Ben's Bells, which has a location now in Newtown. Ben's Bells seeks "to inspire, educate, and motivate people to realize the impact of intentional kindness, and to empower individuals to act according to that awareness, thereby strengthening ourselves, our relationships and our communities."[1]

Too often, we think of kindness as a quality someone either possesses or does not. We admire a kind person as a rare object. We speak of kindness as a random act, something that surprises us precisely because it is unusual, unexpected. Kindness, however, is really a habit, an orientation, something we practice and, indeed, can become better at. Kindness is something we practice in relation to community, and some kindnesses are not associated with any one individual but with a sense of collective purpose. By the time a Ben's Bell is completed, for example, at least ten people will have had their hands in it. Some will have fashioned the clay, others will have painted a bead, still more will have fired and strung them. None of these hands will have known the other hands involved in the final creation—no bell can be made in one sitting—and yet all will have trusted that the next makers will care for it, will seek out its beauty, and will bring it closer to brightening a corner of the world.

At that final staff meeting, as lumps of cold, damp clay passed from hand to hand, we didn't force the connections between sculpting, tutoring, community, and writing. We talked some. But mostly we made tiny clay birds' nests, hearts, peace signs, and pig faces with perfect snouts.

"This was just what I needed," one tutor said.

That's enough.

In her book, *Peripheral Visions for Writing Centers*, Jackie Grutsch McKinney (2013, 81) invokes Jerome Bruner's work to remind us that a story does not "just happen": "Stories . . . shape our lives by how we interpret them, by how we tell them, by what they do." McKinney goes on to tell her own story of taking an enrichment drawing course at a local community college while in graduate school and of learning in that class about the importance of drawing the negative space, a technique that counters the tendency to draw what we see in our heads at the expense of drawing what we see right in front of us. To do this, the artist must "not actually think about drawing the object but [must] instead focus on drawing the space around the object—drawing the negative space" (88). The technique changes how we see and what we see; it calls attention to the dimensions beyond the immediate object and positions that object differently in its own space and in our field of vision.

Dan is a talented, natural illustrator. When I feel low, he searches for a slip of paper wherever we are and passes it over to me. I write down two numbers, any two numbers, and pass the paper back. He regards it, repositions it, fifteen degrees left, twenty degrees right, scanning for possibilities. Then, he puts pen to paper and starts to work, incorporating the numbers into a cartoon face. By the time he's done, the numerals have been transformed, invisible unless you know what to look for.

Around the police department, he became known for his wry, ephemeral observations of police life, rendered on a chalkboard in the briefing room and, when called upon, for his more permanent memorializing of fellow officers who had passed away. When a sketch artist course was offered by a local police department, Dan enrolled and became certified.

What neither of us considered when he began the course, what was revealed only in the process and, later, as he began his official sketching, was how important good questions would be to recognizable representations. Certainly, sketch artists need to be able to draw; but they also need to be able to draw *out* the victims or witnesses, to draw language and image *into* dialogic relationship, the eraser as essential as the charcoal to shape and re-shape the rendering.

UNPLANNED OBSOLESCENCE AND INSTITUTIONALLY-LITERATE LIVES

"Who am I? Whose am I? Who am I called to be?" These are foundational questions on the campus of Fairfield University, the Jesuit Catholic university that has been my professional and in many ways my personal home for more than twenty years. Traces of these questions are everywhere on campus, underpinning the University mission statement; organizing the residential learning communities; guiding our local, national, and international community service. Increasingly, as I move through my days on and around Fairfield's grounds, I see in my mind's eye a landscape filled with people, even when knocking around campus on the quietest of days. I am beginning to realize that I have dwelled, am dwelling, deeply in this one (for me) somewhat unlikely location, in many different roles. I wonder what has mattered, what will have mattered, about my presence in this place where I have devoted so much of my life.

When I accepted the position at Fairfield, I joked that I was relocating to "the purple state," my only frame of reference for Connecticut being its color on those elementary-school maps of the fifty states. I had never been to Connecticut, didn't in fact know anyone who had ever been to Connecticut. My knowledge of the Jesuit tradition was similarly restricted, limited to the connections between critical pedagogies and liberation theology, with their shared commitments to what the Jesuits describe as "the preferential option for the poor." I am fairly fluent in Ignatian-speak now, but when I arrived at Fairfield, I was largely unprepared for the institutional literacy learning curves that lay ahead those first few years. They were everywhere—from figuring out how to read (and write) minutes, how to follow (and make) motions, how to prepare applications and reports, how to evaluate job candidate materials, how to participate in faculty governance, how to make a successful tenure case. The list goes on and on. There was a lot to learn.

Administrators come and go. But faculty remain. That's the counsel I received as I adjusted to my first new dean; and, in certain ways, it is true. Administrators came and they have gone, four or five times over. New administrators have come where once there were none. I remain.

Fairfield's central administrators[2] are concerned about the sustainability of our current model of operations, so much so that the subtitle of our developing strategic plan is, in fact, "Building a More Sustainable Future."[3] Faculty too are invested in the viability of the current model and support the goal of a more inclusive, more affordable college education. But few faculty list the first sustainable principle for a university as

"To build and implement a new business model that broadens our revenue streams and makes our costs more responsive to our articulated priorities." I encounter this language from our Fairfield 2020 strategic planning documents many times as I log into the system through which faculty performance is reviewed, and I realize: We cannot talk about sustainability without talking about faculty. We cannot talk about sustainability without talking *with* faculty. "Sustained merit" is in fact the original term for the default category in our faculty salary distribution system. The faculty sustain. I sit on the university's merit review committee, with its official charge and its secure database and its appeals processes. I log in to the interface and marvel at colleagues who distill a year's worth of teaching accomplishments into a 250-word text box. And then I tab to the next text box for research. And tab again for service. Sustained, sustained, sustained. All faculty are sustaining.

I served on, and chaired, the Faculty Salary Committee (FSC), work that stands as the steepest of my steep institutional literacy learning curves. During my term on the FSC, senior administrators, backed by the board of trustees, brought forward a merit pay proposal that led to a significant restructuring of the full-time faculty compensation agreement.

Our cross-disciplinary group of faculty on the FSC met at least weekly to sift through the data that the university's administrative team would provide, to identify gaps, figure out our questions, set the weekly meeting agenda, and review the various documents under consideration. We met to plan to meet with the administration's representatives. We considered what to do with the information we had, what information we didn't have but should, what information we were unlikely to get but needed to request anyway. As FSC chair, I prepared and gave the reports to the General Faculty, translating administrative positions for faculty and faculty positions for administrators. It was a familiar role.

When I recall my time on the FSC, I am reminded of Deborah Brandt's account of the case of Dwayne Lowery, the line worker who becomes a union leader (Brandt 2001). Lowery's early success in organizing and advocacy was sponsored on the ground at his workplace as well as through professional development opportunities. Eventually, however, the value of the literacy skills Lowery had been acquiring diminished in the face of increasing bureaucratization. Reading about Lowery, I feel for him. Some days, I feel *like* him. Brandt writes, "[I]nstitutions undergo change, affecting the kinds of literacy they promulgate and the status that such literacy has in the larger society" (56).

At the end of our "collegial discussions" (as a private university, we are prohibited from unionizing by the Yeshiva decision and so are frequently reminded that we cannot "negotiate"), we wound up with a three-tiered merit system: Additional Merit, a category that is almost never funded; No Merit, a category (which would be allocated a 0% increase) that can rarely be justified; and the category into which nearly everyone falls: Sustained Merit.

Still, fewer and fewer faculty labor in sustainable positions at Fairfield as elsewhere; on my campus, we are working to ensure that conditions across labor categories converge. To the extent that this is happening, it is less because conditions are improving for part-time faculty and more because they are deteriorating for full-time faculty. Meanwhile, our documents dis-incentivize collective action. Though many tenure-line faculty express sympathy, dismay, anger, and shame at the working conditions for part-time faculty, the part-time faculty on our campus, as on many campuses, remain woefully under-represented in critical discussions, ranging from departmental business to curricular decisions to compensation negotiations. And our documents, along with the historical interpretations of those documents, compose their ongoing exclusion. Administrators view the governance process as slow, unwieldy, confusing. Faculty object to administrative invocation of extra-institutional bodies— benefits consultants, attorneys, "the state"—to justify ignoring, obstructing, or bypassing agreements codified in institutional documents to which faculty view all parties as bound.[4] We bear witness to the decomposition of the texts on which the university was built.

Perhaps this shift is inevitable in an era in which documents are increasingly ephemeral, circulating on a network, landing in an inbox from the disembodied "universityannounce@" or "facultyannounce@" or from simply "Fairfield University" itself, disappearing with the click of a key. In an article entitled "To: You, From: Michael Blitz and C. Mark Hurlbert, Re: Literacy Demands and Institutional Autobiography," the authors begin, "Just a reminder that the agenda for today's meeting will be to find out what literacy demands are and to determine the extent to which they contribute to or constitute institutional autobiography." They gathered all the mail that arrived in their department mailboxes for a year and concluded: "The documents that 'arrive' . . . supply us with little histories in the form of decisions that we have had some/no part in making" (Blitz and Hurlbert 1989, 7–8).

Since 1989, when Blitz and Hurlbert wrote this article, we have experienced a revolution in the means available to our institutions to compose us and our work. Our faces look out from various landing pages, log-in screens, and sizzle sheets, for all the world to see. These representations are rarely within our power to revise, adapt, or delete. Blitz and Hurlbert write of a "visible, audible, and hermetically institutional Literacy . . . which speaks as a shifty subjectivity—shifty because it is both transient and tricky . . . Every literacy demand is, in other words, a minute and momentous pedagogy" (12).

Claude Mark Hurlbert was my dissertation director; I was one of his first doctoral students. It has been over twenty years since the sun-soaked day when he hooded me. Claude retired this past May, and it is hard for me to believe that a whole career has passed between then and now.

What I'm leaving out is this:

I spent seven years as a central administrator, working to advance Fairfield's previous strategic plan, the one positioned now as in desperate need of a refresh. That plan was collaborative and student-centered. It privileged teaching and learning. It capitalized on what I would still argue are Fairfield's "value propositions." In partnership with an inspired set of colleagues, I began to believe that we could not only teach English but actually lead our educational institutions so that people would stop killing each other. That previous strategic plan might now be viewed as stale, well past its due date, but it feels startlingly fresh to me.

As the new strategic plan comes into focus, I train my lens, Sally Mann-style, on the deterioration of various types of literacies that have been sponsored in, through, and by the institution. As Mann walked the perimeter of the body farm, so I travel the footpaths of my own campus, contemplating the composition of the soil. I walk down Bellarmine Road, up the hill on O'Neill Way, and around the corner of Fitzgerald, and I am called back to my first moments as a graduate teaching assistant in a Mississippi master's program, about to embark on one singularly disastrous year of college teaching.

That year began with three hours of professional development—a morning workshop for inexperienced teachers during which time a senior faculty member assured us "The good ones, you can't hurt; The bad ones, you can't help." I remember feeling deflated by that statement, even as I tried to draw on its limited wisdom. I had no transferable framework when faced with the literacy demands of teaching: constructing a syllabus, planning a unit, designing assignments, grading a set of papers, even maintaining a grade book. Every task seemed somehow free-floating in its own universe, and every need was pressing, not the least of which were the needs of students. Needs that appeared to be disconnected from the papers they were supposed to be writing but that somehow kept insinuating themselves into the work of our class: One student threw a chair at one of his group members. Another came to class repeatedly visibly beaten but certain she had asked for it. And then, one went home for Thanksgiving break, loaded his shotgun, put it in his mouth, and never came back.

I had taken home a lot of student writing over Thanksgiving break, so I had nearly a complete writer's notebook of that student's experiences, right up until the week he killed himself. What had been an unremarkable, undifferentiated section of first-year writing was now a topic of significant interest among various administrators. They wanted all of his writing. They wanted the syllabus, the assignments. They wanted to talk to me. Suddenly, everyone wanted to know what had been going on in my class.

What to say about the sponsors of my institutional literacies at that particular moment in my career? I can't recall anyone expressing concern about how I was being constructed in this scenario, or how my own entrance to the profession I had seemingly chosen was being configured by not only the terrible loss and the questions I now had about what I could have noticed, but also by the institutional gaze that was trained on me. I don't think faculty and administrators were wholly indifferent; I think that they too were wildly underprepared: "The good ones, you can't hurt; the bad ones, you can't help." Certainly, I learned how powerful institutional documents could be, how they could stand (in) for (and against) individual institutional actors.

When I entered the doctoral program at Indiana University of Pennsylvania, just shy of two years after that initial teaching experience, I knew shockingly little about the place. It felt more like I was entering an academic witness protection program. I leapt at the chance to flee all sorts of personal and professional complications and tuck myself away in the Alleghenies, Harrison Ford style, until things cooled down. I arrived for a five-week summer session, and I stayed for three years. I had no idea that a "Politics of Composition" seminar I took that first semester with Claude would afford me the space to think with others about the relationship of literacy to violence in its many, many forms. I was not ready then to talk about my initial teaching experiences, but I was more than ready to encounter the work of Elspeth Stuckey, of Mary Rose O'Reilley, of Richard Miller, of Claude himself and his then-frequent co-author Michael Blitz, whose work on violence in and around the writing classroom shocks and saddens me still with its contemporary relevance.

I tried and failed then to develop a bullet-proof syllabus, and now it seems neither possible nor desirable to develop a bullet-proof writing program. Violence, and the call to respond to it with compassion, composes much of my professional and personal life, but I have not, until now, connected this lifelong commitment to my first semester teaching, to the sorrowful experience of that terribly troubled class. From Mississippi to Western PA, from New Orleans to Bridgeport and back again. To Lafayette, LA, where my mom and dad used to go to the movies as a young married couple to escape the summer heat. To Charleston, SC, where my poetry project colleague and collaborator taught before moving with her husband and young sons to Newtown, Connecticut, six months before the shootings at Sandy Hook. To my own grown-up hometown of Milford, CT, where one of my husband's fellow officers killed himself on Father's Day. I set aside the drafting of this essay to attend the wake and the funeral, to accompany Dan, who accompanied the casket, from the funeral home to the church to the gravesite to inter the remains.

WAYFARING STRANGERS, WAYFINDING COMPANIONS

Fairfield University is essentially a gated community. No one passes through it on the way to anywhere else. A guard station marks the main entrance and warning signs mark the others. The campus is impeccably manicured, with benches where you can sit beneath the willows that dip into the pond (as long as you don't feed the wildlife), stretch out on green grassy knolls (as long as you don't bring your dog), and explore the trails leading to the Zen garden (as long as you smile for the cameras and park only in designated areas). It seems that all institutional literacies should be similarly composed. We go *to* Bridgeport or New Orleans or El Salvador or Cuba, but we're not really supposed to carry those places back with us.

When I returned from a quiet afternoon of writing on campus, Dan pulled up one of our small local circulars and pushed it toward me. The headline read "Cops: Man hangs self in woods near Fairfield U" and the final paragraph confirmed: "Officers began to search the immediate area, including the woods on the university property. It was there they discovered the man's body, hanging from a tree" (*Fairfield Citizen*, June 24, 2015).

People are in pain, in Newtown, yes, and in New Orleans, true, and in El Salvador, certainly, but also on our own campuses. Right here in front of us. That pain presents a *problem*, as it insinuates itself into the perceived real work of the institution. Can we acknowledge that our experiences with pain anywhere should render us more, not less, capable of responding to it everywhere? Compassion, it seems to me, is an infinitely renewable resource.

It is difficult to draw the connections, as I would like to, between violence in our communities, violence on the edges of our campuses, violence that makes its way into our classrooms, and the violence implicit in our institutions' refusal to acknowledge the power they mask through the increasing disembodiment of our educational enterprise. We are experiencing the deterioration of the value of expertise, and shifts in the value of academic literacies writ large and as they have been historically practiced. The central consolidation of power, the control of information, along with the simultaneous denial that such practices are operative: These are contemporary literacy tests; we should make no mistake about that. In too many places, in too many ways, we are failing them.

Near the end of the academic year, an email message with the subject line "To the General Faculty from the President" arrived. In it, the President informed the faculty that the Faculty Salary Committee and the administration had reached agreement on compensation for the coming year. This was good news and, even though significant changes to benefits loomed large, contract terms were relatively favorable. All faculty were sustaining.

The President's email message also announced that the Senior Leadership Team would be recommending changes to the process for determining salary and benefits. The message undercut the successful conclusion of the year's reasonably equitable compensation agreement by positioning salaries and benefits as an institutional *problem* to be solved. The President noted that salaries and benefits are the university's largest operating expense—sixty-five percent of the annual budget!—as though it were self-evident how concerning this figure should be. I learned, in the days to follow, that I was not the only person who read this figure and thought, *So?* What else would the university's largest operating expense be? What else *should* it be? What is the target percentage, and why? We were told that the current levels are unsustainable, but many of us wondered, *What else is a university made of?*

The President didn't anticipate any of these questions in the end-of-the-year remarks he gave to the General Faculty only a few weeks before circulating this email. Instead, he called on faculty to be civil in the face of potentially radical transformations of our work/lives, as the values on which we have bet our and our students' futures are rendered obsolete. Perhaps he too is reeling, as many of us are. I questioned the potential chilling effect of such calls for civility. The President responded briefly from the floor of the meeting and more fully in a personal email message to me two days later. It was unclear whether his message invited a response from me or foreclosed one. I responded. He did not reply.

Meanwhile, organizational announcements continued to pop into our inboxes—new vice-president positions; the promotion of a vice-president to provost; the promotion of a dean to associate vice president and of a director to dean; searches for faculty lines failed and were cancelled; faculty salaries were re-purposed—for what new purpose, no one can quite say. Recommendations from faculty who run programs, including those of us who run writing programs, were met with a thin Fairfield line about "the institution's best interests" and a corrective that we were somehow not the ones from whom such recommendations would come.

As a university leader during a time of rapid organizational change, I played and will continue to play my own role in complex decisions. I do not exempt myself as an actor in these institutional scripts, either as someone who experienced or as someone who inflicted pain. Even now, I co-direct a first-year writing program that took more than a decade to build and faces "significant reorganization," a euphemism for the potential elimination of even the most radically contingent positions on our campus, those of our adjunct writing instructors. None of us is in an enviable position. I am implicated. We are all implicated. As our institutions shape and shift, we struggle to make sense of these changes. Perhaps pain is an inevitable part of that picture. If so, we can at least acknowledge that it is simultaneously regrettable. We can gesture toward healing. We can speak to each other's humanity.

I joke that it took me a year's worth of General Faculty meetings to realize that, when we call the question, we actually stop talking about the issue. The calling of the question seemed to me to be just the beginning. I know now that in many ways it *is* just the beginning, that many questions still follow the calling.

As I put the finishing touches on this section, I participated in a workshop for the Connecticut Writing Project–Fairfield. Our CWP director tweeted out a photo of our group, and it was re-tweeted by "Fairfield University." That night in my inbox was a message from a long-ago-graduated student, Gary. I supervised his honors project, which explored, among other things, the concept of the trace and the question of remains. Through that project, we first encountered Sally Mann's work, on a field trip to the Houk Gallery in New York City for an exhibition. It seemed prescient work to have been doing, when Gary's father passed away later that year, only a few weeks shy of Gary's graduation from Fairfield. The message that arrived from Gary in response to that tweet read, "i'm sitting down, kids asleep, light up my computer to do a few last things, and run across a tweet featuring you. for a brief moment i flash back to this very special time where questions were as valuable as answers. what a rare thing."

A GATHERING PLACE

I got a slow start on a warm Friday morning in late October, so I was still padding around the kitchen with a mug of hot tea when my phone beeped a security alert from the campus network:

> To the University Community:
>
> There have been several threats made to individual schools in the Town of Fairfield. There have been no threats made to either Fairfield University or Fairfield Prep.
>
> As a precaution, all University gates are closed. All visitors to campus are to be directed to the main gate on North Benson Road. Please be sure to have identification available if you are leaving or arriving to the campus. All operations of the University will continue as normal. We will keep the community updated.
>
> Thank you for your cooperation.
> The Department of Public Safety

At first, I barely gave the message a second glance. Then I decided I should forward it to Dan. He replied, "Haven't heard this. U going into school?"

"Yes," I texted back. "I have meetings this afternoon. I'm sure it's precautionary."

Getting to campus took longer than usual, because all gates were closed except for the main entrance, and arrivals were asked to present university ID. I played stop-and-go behind an impatient Toyota 4Runner with an NRA sticker on the back windshield.

Once in my office, I saw a new message:

Update to the University Community,

There have been no incidents reported in the Town of Fairfield and no additional threats have been received. Fairfield Public Schools, as a precaution, will be closing early today. Fairfield University is currently serving as a gathering space for parents from the community. We anticipate that to be a temporary situation. Parents who are currently on campus will be receiving instructions shortly to return home to receive their children following the early dismissal.

All University entrances will be open shortly. University operations continue as normal.

Thank you for your patience and cooperation.

The Department of Public Safety

What should have been a benign, even reassuring, update instead triggered memories of the staging areas in Newtown, where parents rushed to meet their children, some of whom, we know, never joined them. I was struck by the disembodied voice in these alerts. Who exactly is The Department of Public Safety? All other university and organizational announcements appeal to the authority of the (purported) authors—The President, The Provost, The Vice President of One-Thing-or-Another. But these DPS signature lines were singular in their rhetorical appeal to the authority of the institution.

A gathering space. Let's all gather ourselves.

For lockdown drills in our own school district, Dan now assumes the role of intruder. He is as taciturn as I am talkative, rarely offering many details of the eerie quiet in the otherwise cheerful halls, the drawn shades of the otherwise colorful classrooms.

At home, he takes the news in slowly, old-school style, with three and sometimes four daily papers delivered to the end of our driveway. He sits quietly in the same spot on the couch, a cup of coffee beside him, and pores over them first thing in the morning and again, with the ones that arrive after he leaves for work, just before dinner. One evening, he paused on a photo above the fold of our local paper, a picture of a brownie troop that had visited the local police station. A dozen tiny faces were crowded behind the bars of one of the holding cells. I watched him regard it, saw something in his face. "What?" I asked.

He described the recent drill at our elementary school. "You have to try every door," he said. One after another after another. Grab the handle, press it down, lean in. Locked, locked, locked. "Then," he said, "I go to the next door. Grab the handle. Press it down. And it opens."

He walked into the darkened classroom, pulled his flashlight from his duty belt, and scanned the room until it landed on the pile of children huddled in the back corner, pressed against their teacher, who in the frenzy of shutting and pulling and shushing and gathering had failed to secure the lock.

"Baby birds," Dan said. "That's what they looked like. Baby birds. That's what Lanza shot."

The day after Thanksgiving is my favorite day of the year to write. It is a funny thing to have—a favorite writing day—but maybe other readers and writers will understand. Force of habit being what it is, I checked email (let's be honest) as soon as I got up. A few belated auto-generated expressions of gratitude, a warning that my NetID Password would expire soon, the *NYTimes* daily digest, and one university announcement, sent at 8:39 a.m., with the subject line "Faculty and Staff Recommended Training for Violent Intruder on Campus." The message listed 4 upcoming training sessions and the following enjoinder: "*It is strongly encouraged that all Faculty and Staff attend one of the sessions.*"

Black Friday it was.

I walked into the kitchen to fix a bowl of cereal and saw a sticky note with Dan's handwriting on the morning paper—"This woman went to LSU :-("—on a story about a local murder-suicide. Next to the stove he had left a business card with a smiling family photo: "Thank you for what you do each and every day! You are appreciated! In Memory of East Hartford Police Officer Paul S. Buchanan #208 who died by suicide on March 12, 2013." On the back of the card, we were asked to "read Paul's story" on lawenforcementtoday.com and watch the YouTube video, "Breaking the Silence of Police Suicide." So I did.

This was all a sobering start to my favorite writing day.

Whenever Dan comes home from work with a story of encountering a gun, it feels alive to me. In a forgotten backpack, jostling around with a laptop, a notebook, and an array of assorted school supplies; in a foot pursuit, where a glint of steel catches a ray of sunlight as it is flung into the brush; at the scene of a domestic, where a woman screams while a man—pacing frantically, huffing and puffing, a pistol's butt visible in his waistband—lurches toward Dan, yelling, "Take it, take it, take it!"

When I think of the over 50,000 victims of gun violence each year in this country,[5] I sense a trace of this exchange in nearly every one of them, a fleeting moment when the shooter might have appealed to someone—a cop, a friend, a retailer, a manufacturer—to take it, take it, take it.

I hear you, all of you.

Guns don't kill people. People kill people. Eleventh-grade research-paper logic. It's more complicated than that. "It is neither people nor guns that kill," writes Bruno Latour (1994, 34). "Responsibility for action must be shared among the various actants." In a society where five-year olds shoot three-year olds and two-year olds shoot their parents, is it magical thinking to assert that guns don't kill people? Is it depraved indifference to enable the violence to continue? "To believe in rhetoric, then," Paul Lynch and Nathaniel Rivers write, "is not to assert anything, but to commit to seeing things through, to go all the way in following the networks" (Lynch and Rivers 2015, 6).

In many circles, even among my most progressive friends, taking on gun control as an issue, as *the* issue, is a tilting-at-windmills proposition. An unwinnable position. The conversation quickly shifts to increased safety measures and mental health dollars; energy coheres around the most unlikely scenarios—active shooters in schools, movie theaters, malls. Episodes of urban violence, suicide, and intimate partner violence—the places and spaces where access to guns is likely to have the deadliest outcomes—simply accumulate. Friends and colleagues committed to reducing gun violence advocate for stricter background checks, assault weapons bans, and smart-gun technologies. Local affiliates of My Brother's Keeper and Ceasefire challenge communities to address the root causes of violence. As I research how to participate in efforts to reduce gun violence, questions pile up, one on top of the other. I experience the frustration so many express: Where do we start to make it stop? Perhaps we need to rethink our questions. We need to try. I am going to try.

I started to read Latour. I am not done reading Latour. I will not be done reading Latour by the time I finish this essay. But I started. And I read.

I read with the eyes of a nonspecialist, without expecting to find answers so much as to construct better questions. At the end of *War of the Worlds*, Latour (2002, 40) in fact suggests this methodology when he writes, "[T]he notion of construction could serve as a lingua franca for beginning to understand each other. . . . Here is where negotiations could begin: with the question of the right ways to build."

I read as Latour exposes the limits of rationalism, the disembodied universality of scientism, and the ethnocentrism of all forms of modernism, as he expresses skepticism of straight lines and binaries.

I read as someone whose all-operations-continue-as-normal hinges each and every day on whether a gun is part of the scene, whether a gun remains in a waistband. Or a backpack. A holster. Under the driver's seat. On whether it is flung or pointed.

I read as someone who has experienced, is experiencing, the ways technologies change how we move through the world. And as someone who teaches others (at times) to accommodate and (at others) to embrace these changes. I write on the smooth, shiny surface of a slick, sleek MacBook Air, my instrument of choice bearing a certain materialist resemblance to the other objects about which I write.

Why Latour? In part, certainly, because he is having a moment in rhetoric and composition studies. (See, for example, Lynch and Rivers 2015.) Because a colleague, while standing in the doorway of my office, made an offhand remark about the doorknob as *actant*, following it with a reference to Latour. And because, to explicate his theory of mediation, Latour offers an extended analysis of guns and humans' complicated relationships to them.

"What does the gun add to the shooting?," Latour asks. He then offers the materialist position ("everything") and the sociological position ("nothing"). He describes these two responses as "absurdly contradictory":

> No materialist claims that guns kill by themselves. What the materialist claims is that the good citizen is transformed by carrying the gun . . . As to the NRA, they cannot maintain that the gun is so neutral an object that is has no part in the act of killing. They have to acknowledge that the gun adds something, though not to the moral state of the person holding the gun . . . With a gun, one kills better, but at no point does it modify one's goal. (Latour 1994, 31)

Latour reveals the problem of the either/or position, forwarding what he calls a "third possibility": "[T]he creation of a new goal. . . . I call this uncertainty about goals *translation*" (32).[6]

One afternoon, as Dan walked through headquarters, he was waved into a meeting of The Brass. They were ordering new equipment, and they wanted to get a look at his taser, which was affixed to his duty belt by a strap that left it swinging loosely at his left side. Not ideal. "Walk us through how you draw it," one said. Dan began to demonstrate, narrating with an I-would-do-this, then I-would-do-that. Impatient, one of the Commanding Officers stopped him and said, "Look, when you have used it in the past, how have you drawn it?"

"I haven't ever used it," Dan said.

Translation. A third possibility. The drawing of the negative space. What is our goal here?

WAIT FOR ME IN THE SKY

The deadline for the first draft of this essay was January 1. I had been working on it steadily throughout the semester break. The year was coming to a close. The essay was not.

My family gathered between Christmas and New Year's. The Florida contingent arrived in Connecticut, travelling straight up I-95. We were enjoying the full house—the cooking, the storytelling, the roughhousing—so I didn't hear my phone ring. I saw only that I missed a call from a colleague and checked my voicemail.

December 30, 3:01 p.m., 18 seconds: "I'm calling to share some very sad news with you."

I returned the call and learned that a dear friend and colleague had been killed, along with her husband, her mother, and her brother. Gisela and her husband José had flown that morning from Connecticut to Florida to join family for New Year's. They had just been gathered at the airport by her brother, accompanied by her mother, were heading down I-95 in Miami when they were involved in a head-on collision with a wrong-way driver. I had read about the crash earlier in the day, trending on social media. The shock of recognition as I put these two separate worlds together doubled me over. My family rushed to me. "What happened? What happened? What happened?" I finally choked it out. They dispersed, and I sat alone in the dark, trying to gather myself.

Little more than an hour later, a university announcement came in with the subject line "Heartfelt Condolences—A Message from the University President." It was indeed as heartfelt as any I have ever read. It closed with an assurance that details about a memorial service in the spring would be forthcoming and an acknowledgement that certain administrative matters would need to be addressed once university operations resumed. As I was reading this announcement, one more message came in, from Higher Ed Hot Topics, advertising "Guns on Campus 2016: Laws, Policies, Politics, & Conceal Carry," a webinar available to your entire staff, complete with event recording and materials for $389. An industry is born.

A day later, on New Year's Eve, my family went out to dinner, and we were joined by a friend of my father's, who offered her condolences on Gisela's tragic death. "Your father was very concerned," she said. When I responded that yes, I had been very upset, she looked at me gravely.

"They all thought it was Dan," she said. He had been working when the call came in. "They thought something had happened to Dan."

We rang in the New Year quietly at home. Ryan Seacrest chattered in the background, but everyone was mostly asleep in front of the TV. Dan had worked all day that day. He would work all day the next. This was a late night for him. I looked over, and he was passed out in the recliner as midnight drew near. I decided to let him sleep through the ball dropping, the ringing, figuring it would still be the new year whenever he woke up.

Tucked into a corner of the couch, the dog in my lap, I scrolled through various social media sites. On Facebook, Gisela's page had become an unofficial memorial site, as friends all over the world mourned her loss. One colleague, a fellow mass media communication theorist, said:

> You once wrote—about Facebook memorials no less—that "the dead never really die; rather they perpetually remain in a digital state of dialogic limbo." Rest in peace, my friend. Hope you can hear our words, our love; I will never forget yours.

Someone dedicated the last five minutes of the year to her; one friend told her that her death had "overwhelmed the networks." Another's plea was auto-translated as "wait for me in the sky."

Meanwhile, over on Twitter, Connecticut state senator Chris Murphy had wrapped up his New Year's Eve "tweet-a-thon" of every single mass shooting of the past year. The tweets ranged from somber ("a bloodbath") to cheeky ("An unprecedented 9 day break!"). For all of his efforts—372 tweets, rolled out over 2 hours—most of his tweets garnered fewer than 100 re-tweets, leading *Washington Post* reporter Amber Phillips (2016) to conclude, "In many ways, Democrats are trying to force the issue on a public that isn't committed to the cause—even among those who agree with them."

By New Year's Day, much information was circulating about Gisela, about her family, about the accident, about its aftermath—on local TV in Connecticut and Miami, in the newspapers, on social media—but very little of it involved any official university channels. Nothing since the Heartfelt Condolences. Our emergency procedures tell us to presume that the university is open, the default position is open, but we all know, between Christmas and New Year's, the default position is closed. The university is closed. Its people are scattered. Few characteristics define academics more than the fact that their families and friends are far-flung. They were gone, we were gone, yet still looking to gather. So gather we did, as best we could, virtually and face-to-face, in people's homes, at a community center, at favorite restaurants and bars. A memorial service was being planned, but it was still weeks away. Campus reopened on January 4, but no gathering space was readily identifiable. Apparently, this devastating loss does not fall into the category of critical incident. There is no threat, no active shooter, just a gaping, collective wound. As I drove to campus on that first morning back to work, I recognized the too-familiar pang of the depths of grief. I dragged my wheels along the way, driving past Gisela and José's house and stopping by my favorite coffee shop, where I spent a few hours writing. While there, I got an email message from a colleague. She began, "I'm in at school, where people are just as sad as you would imagine." What more is a university made of than its people? Not much, as it turns out.

Gisela was an activist. I can't think of anyone who loved life more and fought harder to ensure that everyone could enjoy it. She was fiercely committed to the principles of social justice and to the power of the people and of a free press to bring injustices to light. She in fact had the last two postings on the Fairfield AAUP Faculty Welfare Committee's (FWC) Facebook page: the first, a post from mid-October entitled "Situation with Jan- itorial Workers," alerting FWC members to important changes to the university's custodial staff's working conditions; the next, a post from early December entitled "Victory," in which she praised her FWC colleagues and the staff at *The Mirror* (the Fair- field University student newspaper) for holding the university accountable. But this wouldn't have happened without Gisela, who made sure that these circumstances were made visible.

Even though Gisela was flawlessly bilingual, she would occasionally lament her accented English: "I know if I slowed down, I would be easier to understand, but I don't have time. So," she would say with a shrug and a smile, "People will just have to keep up."

Once, after a going-away gathering for a couple of col- leagues who had taken jobs elsewhere, Gisela stood in the door of my office and said, "I feel like the best people are leaving." Then, without waiting for a response from me, she quickly added, with only a hint of resignation, "Oh well, what are you going to do? We keep going. We keep going."

Gisela and her beloved José found the time and the money, even when both were quite scarce, for good food, good drink, great music, great conversation and great fun with their friends and family close to home and all over the world. As it turns out, they were right to live life wide-open, full-tilt. That these two people, with two of their most beloved people, met such a violent, tragic end . . . at this moment, it feels inconceivable in its scope, comprehensible only in the particulars: Who will replace her on the search committee, the library committee, the this-or-that, who will teach what she taught, translate as she translated, travel as she travelled, generously, indefatigably, joyously, always with students and colleagues in her warm embrace. The spoken and unspoken acknowledgment that no one will. No one at all. And yet, I keep hearing her say, What are you going to do? We keep going. We keep going.

EPILOGUE

My brother and his Jen packed up to leave early in the new year, heading back down I-95 to Florida. The weather was cold but clear, pretty much all the way down. My brother carried down the suitcases and the Christmas presents. I packed up some food for the road. Soon everything was lined up near the door, a .22 in a brand-new soft-sided carrying case with the tags from Dick's Sporting Goods still on it, laid across the top of the bags. The Subaru Forester was packed tight for the long drive, and as they pulled out of the driveway, the outline of the case was barely visible in the rear window. If you weren't looking for it, you wouldn't know it was there.

Take it, take it, take it.

Notes

1. https://bensbells.org.

2. "Central administrators" is admittedly a slippery category. I use it here to designate administrators who have significant decision-making authority and whose responsibilities do not involve routine contact with students.

3. "Fairfield 2020: Building a More Sustainable Future" (2014), http://strategic planning.fairfield.edu/.

4. See, for example, the Fairfield University Institutional Progress Report (2009, 4). Submitted to the New England Association of Schools and Colleges (NEASC) in 2009, it responds to the NEASC Evaluation Team's assessment that governance is "a concern for the university."

5. All gun violence statistics are drawn from the Gun Violence Archive: www.gun violencearchive.org.

6. Latour cites Serres's definition of translation as "displacement, drift, invention, mediation, the creation of a link that did not exist before and that to some degree modifies two elements or agents" (Latour 1994, 32).

References

Blitz, Michael, and C. Mark Hurlbert. 1989. "To: You, From: Michael Blitz and C. Mark Hurlbert, Re: Literacy Demands and Institutional Autobiography." *Works and Days: Essays in the Socio-Historical Dimension of Literature and the Arts 13* 7(1): 7-33.

Brandt, Deborah. 2001. *Literacy in American Lives*. New York: Cambridge University Press. http://dx.doi.org/10.1017/CBO9780511810237.

"Cops: Man Hangs Self in Woods Near Fairfield U." 2015. *Fairfield Citizen* 24 June: n.p. Web. 25 June 2015.

Fairfield University. 2009. "Fairfield University Institutional Progress Report, December 2009." Web. Accessed 1 August 2015.

Fairfield University. 2014. "Fairfield 2020: Building a More Sustainable Future." http://strategicplanning.fairfield.edu/. Accessed 21 Jun 2015.

Hafera, Alison R. 2007. "Taken in Water: The Photograph as Memorial Image in Sally Mann's *Deep South*." Thesis. Chapel Hill: University of North Carolina.

Hugo, Richard. 1992. *The Triggering Town: Lectures and Essays on Poetry and Writing*. New York: W. W. Norton and Company.

Latour, Bruno. 1994. "On Technical Mediation—Philosophy, Sociology, Genealogy." *Common Knowledge* 3 (2): 29–64.

Latour, Bruno. 2002. *War of the Worlds: What about Peace?* Trans. Charlotte Bigg. Chicago: Prickly Paradigm Press.

Lynch, Paul, and Nathaniel Rivers. 2015. *Thinking with Bruno Latour in Rhetoric and Composition*. Carbondale: Southern Illinois University Press.

McKinney, Jackie Grutsch. 2013. *Peripheral Visions for Writing Centers*. Logan: Utah State University Press.

Miller, Richard E. 2005. *Writing at the End of the World*. Pittsburgh, PA: University of Pittsburgh Press.

O'Reilley, Mary Rose. 1993. *The Peaceable Classroom*. Portsmouth, NH: Heinemann.

Phillips, Amber. 2016. "What Senator Chris Murphy's Mass Shooting Tweet-a-Thon Tell Us [*sic*] About the Gun Control Debate." *The Washington Post*,

January 2. https://www.washingtonpost.com/news/the-fix/wp/2016/01/02/what-sen-chris-murphys-mass-shooting-tweet-a-thon-tell-us-about-the-gun-control-debate/.

Acknowledgments

This essay began with invitations—to participate in and write about the poetry projects, to speak at IWCA/NCPTW and CWPA conferences, to consider pulling all those thoughts together and shaping them into their current form—and I hope it stands as a reminder of how important invitations are. So these acknowledgments begin with thanks to my poetry project partners: Carol Ann Davis, Nels Pearson, Peter Bayers, Bryan Crandall, Colin Hosten, Ann Marie Donnelly, Lea Attanasio, Charlotte Pecqueux, Molly Gregory, and the students, writers, teachers, counselors, and family members who support our programs; with thanks to Richard Miller and participants in the Rutgers Immersive Course in Experimental Writing; with thanks to 2015 IWCA/NCPTW conference co-chairs Melissa Ianetta and Brian Fallon and 2015 CWPA officers Susan Miller-Cochran and Heidi Estrem; with thanks to *WCJ* co-editors Michelle Eodice, Steve Price, and Kerri Jordan and *WPA* co-editors Barbara L'Eplattenier, Lisa Mastrangelo, and Sherry Rankins-Robertson for publishing the original keynotes and for permission to re-mix the previously published work here; with thanks to Neal Lerner and Rita Malencyzk, who kept other writing projects on track to encourage this one's forward momentum; and with thanks to Michael Spooner, Darrin Pratt, and the editorial staff and anonymous reviewers at Utah State University Press/University Press of Colorado.

Members of my writing group at Fairfield have taught me about indebtedness, kinship, sacrifice, and forgiveness; and for that I thank Bob Epstein, David Crawford, Dennis Keenan, and John Thiel. Members of my Fairfield WSN (Women's Support Network) mark occasions for celebration, commiseration, and consolation; and so my final thanks go to Betsy Bowen, Robbin Crabtree, Helen Kropitis, Kathy Nantz, Emily Orlando, Marcie Patton, Susan Rakowitz, Mariann Regan, and Renée White.

About the Author

Beth Boquet is professor of English and director of the Writing Center at Fairfield University in Fairfield, Connecticut. She is the author of *Noise from the Writing Center* and co-author of *The Everyday Writing Center: A Community of Practice*, both published by Utah State University Press.

Current Arguments in Composition

Utah State University Press's Current Arguments in Composition is a series of short-form publications of provocative original material and selections from foundational titles by leading thinkers in the field. Perfect for the composition classroom as well as the professional collection, this series provides access to important introductory content as well as innovative new work intended to stimulate scholarly conversation. Volumes are available in paperback or ebook form.